STRANDS *the* LENGTH
of the wind

John Smith

For Ardeth

from one Smith to another

John Smith

Nov. 14/97

RAGWEED
THE ISLAND PUBLISHER

COPYRIGHT © JOHN SMITH, 1993

"Just as recapitulation" and "The fourth wall" appeared in
The New Poets of Prince Edward Island (Ragweed Press, 1991).

*Ragweed Press acknowledges the generous support
of the Canada Council.*

COVER PHOTOGRAPH :
Camera Art, Charlottetown

PRINTED AND BOUND IN CANADA BY :
Les Ateliers Graphiques Marc Veilleux Inc.

PUBLISHED BY :
Ragweed Press
P.O. Box 2023
Charlottetown, P.E.I.
Canada C1A 7N7

DISTRIBUTED IN CANADA BY :
General Publishing

CANADIAN CATALOGUING IN PUBLICATION DATA :
Smith, John, 1927–

    Strands the length of the wind

    Poems.
    ISBN 0-921556-38-1

I. Title.

PS8587.M55S77 1993   C811'.54   C93-098543-5
PR9199.3.S5516S77 1993

To Matthew and Lena
my parents
in memory

———————————————

CONTENTS

PART ONE

... *from branch to branch* ...

PART TWO

... *the more desired* ...

PART THREE

... *soft etches* ...

PART FOUR

... *a season of flowering galaxies* ...

PART ONE

*... from branch
to branch ...*

Every sign

Every sign is an evasion: in revealing, it conceals;
in defining, it misses the mark, deliberately,
or by some glitch in the index of refraction. The pain is there
always, but overcome by oxygenation,

body-contact, burn of the sun, needle-drip
of nepenthe in the vein. Breath comes hard: for each
measure of air you have to evolve from the seabed,
but for long stretches of time you can forget all that

and go on structuring the silence with fractal-generated
clouds of incense changed as soon as formed.
What is actually out there, beyond the limits

even of speculation, is answered just by the way
a particular species brachiates from branch to branch
through a forest into which you need never intrude.

THE WIND IS

The wind is in everything. Not just in the leaves.
The rocks thrum, their strike-planes shiver; joints
of the oaks wrench open. It's something as much
in the style of the stalker as in things themselves

or the actual gusting of the wind.
A moment like this can give identity
to a whole culture. Any one of a vast
number of metaphors is true enough to sustain life

for scores of generations. It finds its way, not just
into the meanings of words but into the music of speech:
the air gets harder to breathe in any other way.

Then comes invasion, plague, or colonial expansion. Waking
and sleeping wheel together again, a new pressure-
flake breaks free, and everything begins to resemble it.

Not only the weak

Not only the weak ones. Sometimes the strong birds too
get huddled out of the nest. You find them flattened by impact,
bare or downy, on the pavement, eyes sewn shut
that will never flash-focus a chrysalis under the bark.

Every conceivable world exists, every path
between two points is taken, with some degree of probability,
every reading of a text takes place, every mutation occurs.
But when the recording engineer sets up equipment at point X,

only one guest stands at the gate, a lone survivor,
the mean free agent of his own adventure of arrival,
as sure a match as can be for the hand extended

to greet and measure him. It is a bird preening, declaring
its readiness for life, it is one of the most elegant of geodesics,
a nucleotide sequence with a future, or you, or the world that is.

A few intersections have been detected,
brief domains where theory is identical with fact,
where surviving villages are legendary sources,
and Fourier expansions of the state-function

occur as birdsong. These are sacred grounds
where oracles spoke and heroes vanished and returned.
After days of labour, transfixions of accord.
There may be similar phenomena not yet recognized:

intimations struck across the grain of the commonly received,
picoflecks at the edge of the visual field,
sets of zero measure in the continuum of consciousness.

Privileged days of a particular solitary walker
may be fossil landscapes rich with origin
lacking only a language to be read by.

Appropriate technology

Appropriate technology allows you to identify
and quantify the system's components, including
those present only in wisps and trills. Displays provide
a holistic profile at any desired amplification.

Simple programs enable you to assess systemic variants
by selectively doctoring the amplitudes of bits and pieces.
For example, a data-run higher in silicates, lower
in aldehydes; higher in arthropods, lower in vertebrates;

higher in beneficence, lower in doctrine; higher in remembrance,
lower in dithering; higher in second-order differences,
lower in summary convictions. The apparatus—

call it (1) a dictionary, call it (2) the genus fiction,
call it (3) a field where a child plays, call it (4) a long
convalescence reading Proust, call it (5) someone's life.

WHAT WAS CONCEIVED

What was conceived as symmetric acquired asymmetry
through exigencies of construction, and further asymmetry
through accidents of decay. In the process, its beauty,
as its uniqueness, grew. Eventually the ancient child

looks like a weathered bristlecone pine on a ridge
barely below treeline. It is at this stage
that some itinerant master, remembering his walk
and luck there, records it with a few select gestures of the brush.

The old cathedral relaxes into a diorama of rubble,
but gives birth to a new generation of venerable monster,
a new aesthetic, a new species of peak encounter.

Old choirs blown to the winds, one has no option
but to write one's own liturgy, and this in turn
sets out around itself its immanent architecture, a sacred space.

THE STROKES

The strokes that compose the bridge do not meet,
but the traveller and his donkey pass over safely.
He cannot remember the bridge nor how one step
on the way led to another, yet here he rests

at a tavern fire warming his hands on a bowl of soup,
secure in the illusion of continuity.
Between the neurons—a scurry of micro-servants,
angels proffering the locks to others' keys,

and all transacted with comforting redundancy.
Many years later we follow this very route,
with swatches of appreciative silks in a backpack.

They match the originals well, despite revolutions
in the hierarchies, and the many children
whose memories still wander the roads far from home

and for whom we sprinkle flour and salt at wayside shrines.

YOU WANTED TO HEAR

You wanted to hear angels sing—to render audible
the mystery that each voice goes a journey of its own
while together they make one will, one end. Here meanwhile
at the other extremity of things, rain beats for centuries

on thin walls, and a woman bends at a lonely instrument. You too,
if you listen with self-surrender, will hear between her hands'
encounters with the strings a drop that falls forever and never
strikes a stone. "Joy is easy," sing your orphan girls, "charity
    and clarity

of spirit, near and now." The woman whose fingers step for me
so lingeringly opens an uncompromising emptiness.
There are mountains in my country as in yours, standing

with their snows above cities floating in image on water
by the winterlight of old paintings. Walking today together
where the fortress once stood, I hear, faint yet sure, another, a new

music neither yours nor mine, deep within, high in the air.

Exodos

" The soup is too hot." These were his first words,
according to legend. Up till then, everything,
as he went on to affirm, had been in order:
there had been no incentive to break silence.

When silence was gone, however, and words kept coming,
one noticed flaws in the crystal that must have been present
already. It was the flaws, breaches of regularity,
that bore information, digital cut/thrust.

Precisely here, signatures erupted, idiosyncrasies of
the actual staking its claim, stating its case,
asserting its difference from thought. Suspicion began,

distinctions, catalogues, mnemonics, enhancements,
        instrumentation,
hypotheses. Digressions too: the mind became a wanderer,
a species seeking a destiny. Out there, the geography

was headstrong, a rival yearning for approval, an estranged self.

IF YOU CAN'T

If you can't by an act of will clear the mist,
your only option, given your passion for tendering
an object, is to study light's improvisations
on the mist itself—to render those, heightening

and deepening whatever contrasts are to be seen.
The genius of the moment exacts its changes. At one time
it was thought acceptable—indeed, it was required—
to imagine what you wanted the mist to hide,

or what you felt ought to be there, obscured
but adumbrated by its own act of withdrawal.
Concentrate on what is now. Mist might not always

prove accessible, nor hand responsive to aerial nuance.
The future may ask nothing that hand or eye
or will or invention can provide—perhaps blindness,

or an inattention able to be taken quite by surprise.

Early morning was Japanese. You could feel the faintly
oatish grain of the paper against your skin. Now fog
has lifted, and beads of rain on the leaves have begun to dry.
Red oaks have taken to rustling, and the garden,

spotted with soft-focus blossoms of sunlight, is beautiful still
but less Japanese. The day shift is on at the Toyota works,
and the monks have become invisible. A special zigzag
headtrip up the watersteps once held the arrangement together.

Now new principles of organization are retraining admirers
to accomplish a comparable stitchery—not forgetting
the old way of stopping on the bridge in a place shifted

by a few inches back or forth from day to day to extract
all values of the variables. How soon it has come to be evening,
and cries of blackbirds from the sedges acquire an undertone

close to a dry brush's rasp on laid paper. What could be monks
coaching unidentifiable apprentices are tending the garden.

ONE-WAY OUTBOUND

One-way outbound, all the streets are empty. Soon
black Mercedes will come, a line of them at high speed.
People know better than to be caught outside their houses.
You are alone, going in the wrong direction, towards the centre.

Where are the colleagues? A moment ago you were gathered
in the foyer. Polite supportive minuets. Alone again
examining autograph scores in the labs, chapels of the old cathedral,
you imagine someone (the press?) asking you why,

why you stay. "It is the seminar," you hear yourself reply
gently, in empty corridors with their smell of chemicals.
Where to now? The renowned maestro—you overheard him mention

a way out. "For him, yes. But for me?" This is not a film
of love between wars. Nor dream-manna for your analyst. This
    is a real
city of pain and beauty from which you will choose never to be free.

THE POSES

The poses of the garden statuary have been with us a long time.
Someone invented them, and we have chosen not to change them.
They maintain a human measure in a world otherwise green.
Scale and articulation are arranged to that effect.

The original master had the advantage of being first on the scene.
He detected these forms by their absence and supplied the need.
Now the imagination would scarcely recognize itself without them.
The untitled works erected in the junkyard are quite different.

They claim to have assembled there without human agency,
insignia of inattention to the workings of chance become endemic,
fits of distraction from the demand for calculated gestures.

Mud from distant fields washed over them in the latest deluge
    has blessed them
with singleness of purpose, a wholeness greater than the sum
    of chunks and sprawls.
Green is sprouting, and in the deeply silted parts a garden
    is being planned.

THE PARTERRE

The parterre, seen from the duke's writing desk, is so cunningly
    designed
that we paying visitors who crisscross the set, growing, diminishing,
aimless as we are, can't but confirm the canonic planes of recession.
His forebears persist in resembling their portraits. They are
    fixed in emblem,

submitting as evidence a marshal's baton or an open volume of Cicero,
dying holding a cup to the lips of a dying comrade-in-arms.
Their stares of inexorable bestness vote for family as model
    of human geography
and political science. A broken pediment above the door in homage

offers a small basket of flowers overturned. In the print room
a shepherd boy sleeps away the ruins of a great idea.
In what has become of the deer park, plebeians expatiate

at will and ease. Out of the clean, damp, protracted smell
of the duke's orangery, fig, citron, cypress and palm defer to us
and bow obligingly to acknowledge our noblesse.

I AM MY OWN

I am my own tradition, rehearse my own old themes.
Who first said I strive to create my origin? That a man
seeks to father the child he was? That later
contrives to know itself as the precondition

of earlier? It's true those parent landscapes replayed
with unmatchable energy the chromatics of a visible planet.
Recent researches take us into elemental particles
whose cave walls seethe with action,

dream surfaces of unstoppably complicating fractal chords.
However demanding, external infinities were easy in comparison:
a wash of aerial perspective, a formula for translucent porcelain,

and you'd fixed them once and for all. Not so
the inner infinities. They crumble open indefinitely—
miraculous multiplying loaves self-creating from within.

THE BEST

The best of them are retrieved from the brink of a despair
that they will ever be. They come back, as it were—
although they have never before existed—with hesitation,
reluctant to test their being, by starts and shifts.

If she had not passed by that day, burning with colours
she had never seen, who would have thought of a begonia garden
in this sunny hollow where the trees retire again
as in the faltering of some earlier interstadial?

However long you stay, thinking of yet one more anecdote
as you hesitate at the door, a fragment of the untold
that will finally illuminate everything, your visits

are brief and few. Look where the road turns. It's there
that a former occupant saw the last of a small, shy animal
who, research convinced him, would have changed the history
    of the planet.

As we see

As we see in this cross-section of the apparatus,
the researcher himself is within the retort.
Its walls are the integrity of the physical elements—
or rather the decision that these elements form the ground

and that there is nothing else. Once you agree
that the world is a stage, actors turn up everywhere,
a great period in the history of drama invites your subscription,
and going to the theatre subsidizes the original metaphor.

The point is that this is not a clockwork orrery
about which a descriptive memo might be written.
The observer himself is in question. That cheeky little

animal leaping from twig to twig lays waste a whole summer.
The celebrant supplants what he meant to adore.
The ontologist's thumbprint gives its grain to everything in sight.

TODAY THEY ARE OFF

Today they are off their game. Is it heat, lack of incentive,
or maybe the absence of a charismatic figure—some young man
new to the hunt—whose presence would articulate their energy?
On sunny days after cold and rain, one is frequently off guard:

living is too easy. Of the ones who come through,
many will be permanently disabled.
Perhaps those about to die are distracted by prevision—
their loved ones in a time of peace years later

visiting the graveyards to be marked out in these orchards
where, in the aftermath of battle, the remains will be buried.
Lapses create your fate, like sudden insights:

you imagine you see a girl walking to church across a field below;
     diverted,
you shift the stick too late, the wing explodes, and your father—
is it your father?—flies to safety sadly over the sea.

AFTER

After they exhausted the aquifers, they abandoned the land.
Where they went, who can say? Perhaps they fought it out
among themselves for the last choleric water.
Perhaps they starved, or their immune systems failed.

Perhaps they lost nerve or were seized by some unopposable
inner violence. Their cities ground away in desert wind's
gritty breath, the earth rested, you surmise.
But earth neither rests nor acts: earth is a cursive cinder,

remnant of universal fire; desert wind breathes nothing.
Rain falls far off, earliest explorer
of fault structures underground. For what will ensue,

appeal to imagination. A pack of grimy nomads,
or family or faction driven into exile, see green in an old arroyo,
camp there, dig, find water. That is a beginning.

For us, consciousness

For us, consciousness itself has become the prime
object of study, only because for them
it had become the supreme condition to be achieved.
High on the terraces they split from shale the first

fauna of early seas. But what mattered was light,
exaltation, the air they breathed, exposure—nothing
that would reach the museums, the journals, the lexicons of form.
Loneliness has brought us back to their abandoned camp.

What evidence remains is a talus of cast-off shards,
its scribbles both picked out and dissembled by mountain grasses,
mountain flowers. Take up these fragments, one

by one, toss them in your hand. That's where it lies—
not in the jagged clastic orthography, but in the heft—
nothing weighable, but gravity itself, the mind,

into which, against all odds, the sea floor rose.

SOPRANO AND TENOR

Soprano and tenor die again at the cliff's edge.
The firing party marches away and a half-moon sets.
More than another *verismo* love affair has ended.
The will to infinitude has been condemned to self-defeat.

To be specific, the Romantic Period has been silenced.
In the typical plot of its fantasies, each age affirms its own
insufficiency. How can a part do justice to the whole?
Each program for life is only a fragment of the life

it seeks to master; each era only an episode
in the history it would crown and redeem. In the cool desert
sand of the end of things, a serpent stirs and strikes,

a lone contemplative, wounded, drags himself to water,
heals as best he can, and a world starts again
with rushes, sun, a few trees, and the brash

cries of red miraculous mating birds.

To perform

To perform the sacrifice is to live again the birth of the chant
that accompanies and specifies its acts. Who was with you
there by the fire? No one. Teacher, butcher, priest,
chanter, victim, vapour, he who is born as a god from the flames

that are god—you are all of these. There is no other.
A circle of ash now. Smoke still rising from a green arc
of boughs. Against them the cloistered fire burnt out.
With that green smoke in your hair you are satisfied

briefly. Time to move on. Dawn rakes ashes
into the grass, throws cold charred sticks into the bush.
A light almost decipherable licks along the line of hills.

Embryo clouds, levitant in blue—their limbs will dance
somnambulant shadows across the valley floor.
Along the great river for thousands of miles, cities

will tumble into being and grain by grain weather away.

I JUST AM

I just am, she says, I am no one in particular.
Even when I think hard, I have no past, no future.
I am an apparition of sun, hot sand,
air that ambers me—just that, no more.

A full half-circle of pure horizon conspires me,
and opposite, only a blanched green graph of dune grass.
As I am, emptied of idiosyncrasy, an uncountable
crowd could inhabit me and not be seen.

In all that anonymous assembly, no memories, no guilt,
no plans, no forebodings, a dreamless sleep.

A pair of plovers, coming in low, barnstorm the tide-reach.
A great blue heron veers offshore, circles for altitude,
and heads inland. I plunge in blue. Jellyfish are galaxies,
and I, one of a trillion trillion quartz grains

washed from a lost orogeny to the bottom of the sea.

In the later work

In the later work he grows impatient with the way things are.
The rendering uncompromised, energy undissembled, a will
   to change
breaks up the surface. There is less land, more sky,
and in the sky, trouble hovers on apocalypse. His rivals

sought vicarious tragedy in foreign places, among rocks
in lands of exaggerated profile. He stayed on the flat
where he had always been, but made it work
with the desperation of the hand in act, the manic eye.

He foresaw the end could not be easy. He knew the rejected,
the hard things that, usurped by facility, had retreated,
would arrive and do what they pleased. He would be there,

with his only belongings in a bag. Best for that last encounter
to go least equipped, to give the most awesome
its chance to leap from the face of the most familiar:

the sea-meadows of his infancy with their towers of cloud.

It would be

It would be a poet's novel. Everything
indwelling in tropes and figures. The last—
no, latest—cry of a scrupulous self-scrutiny
going down to resurrect its dead.

Shadows grew more luminous than sunlight
as autumn advanced. The boy reading
in his shuttered room became to summer
what the writer would be to the life

that would quicken in his hand. How droll
that a line of poplars should release all the memories
of a buried race, and the traveller one day wake

to find himself following nostalgic streets
through cities that could not have been foretold.
The skyshell drops and the bird soars away.

To define a point

To define a point at which to begin, coordinates
chosen at random will serve, however obscure.
Take them as your origin. A structure
can be grown from there. A single moving particle

impelled by a branching formula will multiply itself
indefinitely if need be, or recombining its traces,
meet itself at any specified number of nodes.
The main thing is not to harden the free

play of the dialogue, however digressive
and seemingly out of hand it may become.
If the field traversed grows completely dark

with interlaced trajectories, change the scale:
at sufficient magnification, there will always be
untravelled land rising beyond the frontiers.

SCRUTINIZED, SANITIZED

Scrutinized, sanitized, the cat disappears in a cloud of
zeroes and ones. That's the first phase. Each zero and one
is itself a cat or an anti-cat. These flip over
into each other in an ordered way, creating as they do

a feline wavetrain that, given the right hypotheses,
is extensively researchable. To this add a systematic
random flippery, a skittish table-turning that causes
every signal, even the best, to toss and twist, or tumble out of frame.

This fractious neocortex loops knottily and happily
back upon and through itself, injecting into the everywhere
it makes accessible an unmistakable cat-smell.

So are formed the semi-discernible contours. Underneath,
lies a foamy blather where the real action takes place,
a flash-reactive summer night filled with cats in heat.

CLOSE UP

Close up, this is the most delightful of *jeux d'esprit*:
the birds are happy acrobats, there's a rosy warmth
in everything, the spirit that passed this way worked swiftly
without thought—a triumph of the dilettantesque.

Distance transforms it to a lifetime spent
in hand-to-hand encounter with the most recalcitrant things,
the fault-scarps that in the end triumph over whatever
you can do. There's nothing decorative in such a death.

The geometries available circumscribe what can happen.
In this country, people don't waste energy not accepting
their roles. Yet their happiness is far from superficial.

The detail of life may be commonplace.
The final configuration may look like an idle hour,
but justify the history of a hundred billion suns.

AFTER THEY HAVE GONE BY, THE MIND

After they have gone by, the mind perfects them. Not what they were,
but what, in someone's best interpretation, they aspired to be
is the trace that is chosen to remain. The same thing can happen
to those moments we shared—time and the selective and refining

mind make them more cherishable than they could have known
    themselves.
We said nothing as you lay dying, but held hands for hours
the way we did when we were first in love. The hand itself
is one branch of the mind. It too perfects, and needs no instructor.

Something in us is not content that past or poem be just what it was:
it must live a life of self-transcendence. Out of the old king's
    lust for trivia
came the canons of the sublime. And even them their ruins surpassed.

Nature after art surpasses itself. The city's neurasthenic reflections
in its lagoons create a commonwealth richer than its empire
at the height of power. Memory's atoning makes all things new.

PART TWO

... the more desired ...

THE BIRDS RETURNED

The birds returned so often to the island, to one
particular tract of peat bog, that they lost the hang of
interbreeding with any other race than those
who felt at home with the savour of a special ground-spruce

so thick that a man—but there were no men—
could walk on top of it and not fall through.
Inevitably men arrived—the island was a way station
on the route to somewhere else. Then everything changed—

not by much, but enough to keep wariness
on wing, flying wider circles, landing rarely,
the savour of ground-spruce farther off

the more desired. These are depictions of perhaps the last
breeding pairs. The captions have faded. Stories
tell of a land of one prolific mountain, back

before difference, before things parted from their names.

THEY DID NOT

They did not mean to deceive us. They clearly
believed there were three: being, thought, and language.
Now we think there may be only one—probably not
one of the ancient three—or granted the privilege

radically to vary the point of view, any number at all,
nameable or not. From morning shade in the stoa one looked west
across the agora to the harbour beyond. Foreigners
had arrived on the latest ships. Hyperboreans,

speaking a language of hardwood staves clapped together.
Where such men were concerned, anything was possible.
It has proven so. We have explored the city, now flooded.

Under water, being and thought are inseparable,
and all words sound the same. On deck, ancient wisdom
dries to dust; the many-body problem admits no general solution;

our nakedness rejoices in the life-giving merciless sun.

THE OLD

The old volcanic dome weathered down to a ten-league
square of natural landscape garden. In earlier times the natives
   commonly
never in their lives left its dales and fells. Now a simple
change in the values of a few coefficients, and anyone

who wants to take the trouble can generate an alternative
universe. Somewhere a bird like that may actually be in flight.
There's a special kind of otherness that comes occasionally
into your eyes and makes me think so. The cryptic scores

we leave behind when this world is finished with us cannot,
of course, make up for the loss of a single song, the absent-minded
obbligato to an ordinary household chore. I'm cutting

some corners, but what I mean to say is that the scenery here,
the more it is groined by weather and wonder and love, the more
eloquent and copiously referential the pure equations grow.

Love does

Love does conquer all. But only if we decide that it shall.
And only counter to the weave of appearance. They were right,
the dialecticians of triumphs: of love, of death
over love, fame over death, time over fame, eternity

over time. They too were right, the devotees of love, to defy
devourer death, devourer time, dilettante fame, and in one
proud move to pre-empt the dialectic's end at the start:
love, they said, is eternity's seed, is its own

foregone conclusion, victor by ontological
argument against all odds. Alone in their towers, dispossessed,
awaiting execution or castration, how could the world

get at them, they who had made God love and lost their wills
in His? We have inherited their books. We turn the pages.
There is a candle in the mind whose flame persists and thrives.

MODELLING

Modelling, she read the emotional parameters
with rare distinction. One sees that in the finesse
with which the "attitudes" are struck, however deficient
the talents of the many painters for whom she posed.

Clearly her art was of high assurance, as was her sense
for the suchness of the heroines whose legendary crises she portrayed.
I linger hour upon hour in the empty church unreconciled
to the fall of each least fragment of bone through the interstellar

dust that her flesh is made. Did she as a duchess die happy,
fulfilled? What led her—or is it fiction?—muffled in a black shawl
to the leper house, to patient dropping of water

from a feather on dry tongues? The ruby pendant with the duke's
monogram still seems warm with a few atoms of rose
and pheromone. I will not give up this life, this love.

IT'S THE WHOLE

It's the whole of her life that is giving birth,
not just a stray moment that fluttered into her bed
looking for comfort and dark. Every surge of pain
revives a folk theme long ago stoned into silence or grief.

Three revered colleagues at the kitchen table, weaving,
ravelling, the history of philosophy—and she can't
stand it, has to escape to the bathroom with its orchid
scent and favour. The gradients of the epic curve

have nothing to tell her. The navigational
virtuosity that made her a full professor and brought her
festively to childbed has nothing to do with

the cooing of Hegel's doves. She made herself
with her own steel and silky strands a sailor. Groundswell
falls, heaves. Her cello hums the old cold salt spray.

IF WE COULD ONLY

If we could only de-something or other the blocking agent,
whatever it is, there's a good chance the resultant
state of affairs would ex-, in-, re-, or trans-everything.
No doubt the blocker serves a purpose. Likely

there would be nothing deserving the name of reality
without it. But even to proceed against it hypothetically
could give us a start on a new imperial enterprise.
For this reason, we invented languages and continue

to do so. Breakthroughs they make possible have been
promising from both sides, if we are talking of something
that has only two sides—or indeed as many as two.

We eat well in this part of the world despite these conundrums.
Some would say too well. Clearly we need more reactive edges, tighter
multiplex, fewer casual affairs, more passion with more trust.

Too many bomb-blasts

Too many bomb-blasts have cratered the air. The chorus
chokes on dust. Shutters awry, curtains in tatters.
A piano player repeats old brothel music.
Twilight as of a November afternoon invades the house.

Two people are falling in love for the first time.
For them there is no *fin de siècle* décor.
They are discovering all the right places, tempi,
turns of the stair. For them there is no one else's music.

Animals are lusty and living in forests, on plains,
before the coming of man. Evolution and roses
are going to take a wilder and gentler course.

The pianist will not die of syphilis in a cheap room.
Spare them the benefit of hindsight and reports from the front.
They are planning a new universe. Let them go free.

WHAT CITY

What city are we in tonight, what house, how
does the bed lie? I say we, but I find myself
alone. When did you leave my side? Are you sitting
in the next room, thinking your after-midnight thoughts?

Why should I feel your absence so deep in my body,
in such an unreachable place? You have never been here.
I have imagined you for years, but you have never
come to me. I have never dared to single you out,

to ask you. But you are in the next room now,
pacing the floor, standing at the window, holding aside
the curtain, smoking a cigarette. You have turned on the lights,

reached down from the shelves where they stand—in their
    thousands, I don't
know how many—one of the books about you from long ago. It says
in your young womanhood you were more beautiful
    than summer sea and sky,

your daughters discovered the springs of good, your sons
    were map-makers,
and you grew old and forgot what the poets had said of you.
You are reading this now in an unknown city, and remembering.

THINGS COMMONPLACE

Things commonplace at the time signify in memory,
enfief themselves with inevitability, grow
necessary and irreplaceable. A kiss just here
absently on a cheek may lead in the long run to the difference

between everything and nothing. Less than a kiss: a flight shadow
that flicks across a face, and one doubts that anything passed at all,
but that was the swallow's moment, unknown to itself,
at which the whole course of things rippled, crumpled, flipped
    from turbulence

to laminar flow—or was it the other way round?—and made for
its destiny, whatever its destiny was to be, maybe
to have no destiny, or no destiny but memory

the mother, matriarch of meaning. Somewhere in mountains
graphs cross over and nature becomes art. Somewhere in a program
of random fluctuations in ideal space, the world begins.

You must imagine

You must imagine yourself approaching the place
from three distinct directions at once. The impression
is therefore a full-circle panorama of mountain scene
folded in three and superimposed. Features separate in nature

lap over in apperception, sometimes melting together,
sometimes, with care, distinguishable. Sometimes
the effect is of three different eras in geological time
become synchronic. Once initiated into this

mode of arrival, it is hard ever to be simple
in vision or purpose again. You are son, father,
and epic reader of the meeting; the murdered man,

the murderer, and the actor in his tragic mask. The three
ways always join. You are always drawn by necessity
into a single body that deals death, dies, and knows.

THE SOUND OF

The sound of the shot effaced his final word. As a result,
we don't know what he was aiming at. The dark brother,
an angel guarding a ford across a river, himself reflected
in water? Perhaps a stag of many tines, as before,

had traversed his imaginings. There was supposed to be one word
that explained all others. It had actually been sighted often,
but a convincing report had never been submitted. That last shot,
according to some interpreters, did the job. Come. Envelop me.

I want to forget these things ... No, I know you can't. It wouldn't
be right. I have to work this through—and I will. Am I dreaming
    something now
that made him do what he did, though the act took place perhaps

centuries ago, before it was possible to tape a record?
However the issue be resolved, a permanent pause has filled
everything. I hear that shot still. I hear it in every word.

EARLIER

Earlier, when he imagined women,
he made love to them himself; now,
other men, younger and unknown to him,
become their lovers. This change makes clear

the transition from lyric to dramatic form:
self dies away into something like a neolithic
village it has lived in for years and, self-concerned,
has never acknowledged. Children of these couplings

will go on playing in the longhouses
when bones of the old voyeur, having failed
to achieve the necessary level of abstraction,

lie trodden back into common earth. Rivers
are the music of the trysting places. The fall
even of a single leaf is a spring of wonder, though sad.

THE SITTER'S CONCENTRATION

The sitter's concentration sustains,
withstands, the vehemence of technique.
She is still here after the storm, still
nurturing the chemistry of self-reliance.

Traces of the assault that ravishes
and renders her—these too remain,
now part of her, persuaded to share
her substance, assist her being.

Beyond our field of view there well may be
a violent surround. It may even permeate
the space she occupies, but if it does,

it too, like the hands of her creator
and assailant, has been gentled and transformed:
we read its lonely, turbulent events

as articles of adoration.

What is placed in parentheses

What is placed in parentheses creates its own kind of emphasis,
like women whose destiny was to inspire poets, and who instinctively
knew they must deny themselves to the poets who loved them.
Sometimes I almost overhear you in conversation with a
    correspondent

voice within you. Your hands are swallows on windless evenings,
dipping in flight something undetectable from the sheen of
    summer ponds.
The hands of your confidante are swallows too. Lacily they touch
your arm as you both lean forward over a salad that you share.

Digressions, asides, as-if-nesses, qualifications, let-us-assume-nesses,
stage-whispers, addenda, *sotto voce* pillow secrets—they comprise
a universe in extended slow collision with the unadorned

ordinary run of things. We blunt naturals would embrace—
    and often do—
these softer, alien, intrusive members, these shy visitants that bow
their heads against us and evade question (as you do sometimes)
    so engagingly.

JUST AS RECAPITULATION

Just as recapitulation gets under way, there's an unpredictable
hiatus, the piano locks on a repeated diminished-seventh chord,
and the violin soars and plunges, wounded, in cadenza through
   a bedevilled
waste of keys, with no apparent reference to established themes.

At this point, the great wall—it never kept determined barbarians
   at bay—
having followed an orderly line of ridges, enters dragon country,
bucks and heaves over eaten-out volcanic torsos, lashes
back on itself, uncoils over a last crest, and dives below

sibilant millennia of dunes reaching out of sight. Dreamscapes
tell of its onward passage to an empty city once garrulous with
speculations brought in across the desert—a city, and beyond the city,

valley caves painted the colours of a million solitary
states of mind ... Early birdsong by April window, Sunday
morning when I saw you last. You had just done transcribing a faded

foreign script—first for a hundred thousand years to read
the hymns that brought those celebrants to the world's brink
and opened the intangible for the colonists who were to come.

AT THIS POINT, AN IMAGE

At this point, an image enters the stream, spreads, tears, fragments,
and vanishes. By the time you notice, it's already fast resigning
wholeness and sharp definition. Its moment of perfection can't
be distinguished from other effects of memory: it has become

a valediction for what you saw the instant before you
were conscious of seeing. We rejoice in many things for their
tragic disappearances better than we acquiesce in the habits
and permanent possessions that bestow continuity.

Waking to a farewell kiss, I saw the door closing, and already
knew that that particular angel would never return.
The world is a flower because we desire a flower to be all
the world there is, desire in such need that the flower becomes one
with regret that the world offers itself and falls, broken petals,

before we have learned to love. Out of lost opportunities
comes a metaphysic of fulfilment. Civilization
is a home we have built for these motherless children.
Those who die before birth, denied a breathing life, compose
a society of pure idea. We set places for them at table.

They murmur grace in an undervoice before the meal.

... soft etches ...

Opposite

Opposite a difficult passage, just where you look for
an explanatory gloss, what appears in the margin
is another enigma. When scribes recopy the manuscript,
these marginalia get coerced into the text. After many

recopies, successive generations of periphera
infiltrate the body of the work and displace attention
from what drew them there. You expect me to deplore this
adulteration. I do not. Crystal growth in cavities eventually

creates some of the supreme concentrations of beauty, *scilicet*
truth. Off in the distance, utterly novel figures have been
rising in the sky. Possibly they follow the laws of

an unexplored crystallography, and though they occur
millions of light-years hence, actually start from one of our own
fertile horizons, those erotic soft etches across the retinal interface

that we may never be able—should we ever want to?—wipe away.

IF ANYTHING

If anything's knowable, it's implicit in some
language or other—maybe a language we've already got
and have partially exploited and will never, of course, ever
squeeze all the juice from, or maybe a language we've yet

to devise, or one we might devise but, for whatever accident or
indolence or oversight, never will. There's a mountain's worth
of squirrels out there, each with a colony of mites aboard. The mites
are running with mites too. There are oceans of noise in every

language also—more noise than fish. That's one of the problems: how
to separate meat from brine, with confidence all along cunningly
pre-empted by suspicions that those great positives of darkness,
    the extra-

terrestrials around us, enjoying their ruthless sensibilities,
    may read most
message in brine and laugh away the fish we live on. It's a
glorious day nevertheless, graced by the babble of children,

even in so-called backward villages, and every
stone in every stream, cracked open and looked at tinily
and brightly enough, will startle wavetrains in bystanders
    everywhere.

THE HEART

The heart tries to reenact the sea. In the beginning there is no
heart but the sea itself, one and relentless. The heart is not
within; it envelops. Then comes a great involution:
what is inside stretches out to encompass; what is outside

swallows itself down whole and ends up small and contained,
and beating still, though brief. Some time later, we find ourselves
at the scene. We know something has tried to happen and
    succeeds only
momentarily, but goes on trying. At the sea's edge we know this.

One and relentless, the sea goes on, and the heart, shut in,
    acknowledges
it is the heart only because it tries to reenact the sea.
(In the event of success, there need be no sea but only the heart.)

At this point, you and I are running together along the shore.
We know the heart is a sea of two billion waves and when
they have passed, smashing or soothing, it dies. You do not

become prime minister, for all your adrenalin, and however
glorious the sunset, both our names are written in water.

Here the probability amplitude is close to one: expect, therefore, to find
a particle. Nearby, the amplitude drops steeply to somewhere
    near zero: this
marks the ragged edge of expectation: seldom here will you uncover
the sought-for fossil fern or the girl with grey eyes you have dreamt of.

One rare bird covers the whole of Amazonia. The more intense the
desire, the wider the habitat; the more exquisite the specifications,
the less chance of finding it anywhere. This is the story told by every
transcendental signifier: the more exultantly the signified fills
    everything,

the less apprehensible it will be, and the more magnificently rhetoric
will collapse under the strain. In time, the surface of the continents
grows mossy with such ruins. On evidence like this, visitors

from unadulterated spacetime judge the success of life-experiments.
Some testaments have grown so ecologically sound, they can hardly
    be distinguished
from living species. That woman standing on the doorsill stone—

gentle kin, they come to feed with total trust from her extended hand.

ALL LIGHT

All light is fossil light. It says the earliest moments of a star,
the default of a primary civilization. It fixes the specimen in eternity.
You can saw the petrified log later and polish its cross-section
to art, science, religion, boredom. Or not. The signals

may never get picked up by any other atom. On the other hand,
the spin-flip
of one of a practically unaddable set of orbiting events may catch
the eye
and have a museum built around it. The palaeozoic sea floor
sticks to your shoes in wet weather and leaves traces everywhere.

No food is wasted. The eaters scurry in, bristly with self-importance,
to get it, or it relaxes into something inedible but just as useful.
Most of the others seem to know exactly what they want, even though

they've never encountered it; you yourself are almost always unsure.
The structure of populations constantly alters. The species
that forage a given climatic province are trial

translations of a yet-to-be-accomplished animal design.

ONCE DEVELOPMENT STARTS

Once development starts, it runs fast. We like the heady
feel of it. To keep the rush going, it's not enough
to adopt a policy of change for change's sake.
We've proven that: the production lines mass-produce inanity.

There have to be need, a great idea, sense of direction,
violence, and a conviction of who you are that comes from
having to fight for your life against a committed adversary.
It's rare in history for all these parameters to intersect.

Priests have proven as vested an interest as generals. We've had
    trouble
lately from profiteers in soporifics as much as from loss
of nerve. Ideas abound, but we're no longer sure

we've got a great one. A great threat, however, seems to be
advancing: the biosphere's revulsion against us, our own
hands tormented and transmuted into a lethal genetic field.

At the centre, though, if you can lock on to it—we've
been told often, in one way or another, and sporadically
believe—there's a saving point, full of infinity.

First, They Take Everything

First, they take everything apart. That done, reconstructing
gives them a sense of understanding it. Next move is to disassemble
again, but put the natural parts together with omissions,
repeats, and reversals, or in novel sequence or orientation.

The resulting figures engender organisms that never existed before.
It soon becomes possible, without analysis or synthesis, to breed
similar creatures straight off, expedients that seem to fly,
fully endowed with attributes, from a dot between the eyes.

What begins with a modest zoo of these projections
ends with ambitions to populate the world with them,
at first in company with native species, then replacing them,

finally to make of purely crafted evolutionary lines
a functioning universe wholly without precedent.

What becomes of the given once the totally created world
    takes hold, no one
is here to say. Such a world, if it has already achieved critical mass,
has passed out of range, left no residue, lost interest in answering.

THIS AMPHORA

" This amphora you paint yourself, Psiax. No apprentice
lays hand on this one. It must be the master
or none." I remember, Andokides, because that very amphora
went to the girl with the crooked eye on her marriage—old

Lepton's daughter. He bought it specially. Melitta, her name.
 Gone now,
the lot of them, and the amphora with them probably, somewhere
at the bottom of the Icarian Sea. Do you dream much
of the sea? I do. There's no distinguishing. It *is* my dream,

the sea. And all the deities and adventurers, black-figure,
red-figure, yawn and stretch there with new life. Oh, they're alive,
fizzy with the life of the sun, however faint, that finds

its way into water. It's my life too, and yours, we
old men, the life of sun and sea and waterlogged, rippling
gods. Some day, sea nymphs will find us; we'll be traded in strange

markets, along with our heroes and gods, and neither they nor we
will know anything about it. Can you feel in your hands now,
 Andokides,
that amphora? Spinning still, isn't it? It never stops.

THE VARIABLES

The variables exhibit critical values. This accounts for the notches
found in what once were thought to be counting-sticks strewn around
old camp sites. Natural branchings of a tree and the knots
in planking cut from it are stages in developing

the analogy. When a particular speed is reached, the gear ratio
changes abruptly and automatically. The musical scale records
the ordered sequence of such changes. Between each pair
of correspondents, we find a series of transcendental numbers

to indicate universal—or maybe just culturally significant—
stages in the passage from one end-term to the other. Quite
early, animal and plant species, and the ecological niches
associated with each, appear as variants of a single life-
project. Later, when the species become gods, henotheism
develops as a means of ritually fixing the critical

values involved. Later still, the partitioning of the hadron
into discrete manifestations illustrates the same propensity
for hearing characterizing clicks in anything that can be taken
by displacement to be a spoken language. Some of the children
are blue-eyed, some black-, with several hundred variants between,
each with its unique song of praise and totemic fetish, each bound

into the tragic headband by convolutions of curiosity, awe, and love.

Where do they come from, where do they go, these smoky
figures who change the set between scenes? How do they
conceive themselves, forever in black? Do they wring their motivation
from darkness? Here you see them interlace gaps in the fossil record

between one species and its inheritor. There they are the sudden
    massive stars
that have already disappeared from sight before consciousness
    picks up
traces of their heavy metals in river sand to fashion these curious pins,
these engines. Inevitably, we find ourselves sitting in chairs they
    have placed

in drawing-room or arbour. The positions of the trees and
    columns aptly
turn into the lines we speak. We need them there: without them,
    words
hold back, come dry to the mouth. We're microspliced by the
    twists and turns of

these silent partons, made in the shape of the darkness they move in.
Are they taking their cues from us in some attentive,
    surreptitious way?
They die of recognition. Applause turns them self-conscious,
    disperses them,

their soft hands and feet gloved in nothingness.

THERE'S A PRICE

There's a price to pay for knowledge: the animal dies.
But this happens by remote control and is hidden under
clinical conditions. Some photons get through; these are the ones
that create the pattern. Some are stopped by intransigent tissue;

these are responsible for the mutations that progressively alienate
the host from itself and render it finally unrecognizable.
To send up the masterly crafted brain cells, the rest of the mystery
is resolved into an object. Innumerable surfaces intervene,

none of which is perfectly penetrable. At each such barrier,
information is bought and sold, diffracted, or conjugated
into something equivocal in order to drive a few

molecules through. The lacy granules of illumination that precipitate
from the last solution in the series represent only one of a possible
infinite number of modes of reduction. What struck the first explorers

at the scene of these events was the radical austerity of the moving
parts in correspondence with the unmatchable fecundity of the
    sea outside.

We don't know enough

We don't know enough about long-term effects of small inputs.
It's easy to spot death in an overdose. What's more, we've tracked
the intimate fibres of process as they grow. It's slow growth and slow
decay that defy us. We're surprised to discover that the day is longer

and the moon farther away than when we were confined to tidal
    mudflats
and had no hard body parts. We've lacked means to sample the
    lengthening
and the farthering till now. Are the ultimates—perfection, right,
    identity,
and the rest—getting more or less ultimate as time goes on? We
    don't know.

Will physical constants eventually evaporate? Is love any less
    love than it was,
after all the hard words that have passed between? Are you
    altered and how and
how much according to the number of sunsets you've stayed
    to watch?

There's a rare salt that's been leaching into the water supply, I'm told,
since we began asking these questions. If you believe some
    predictions,
in the long run the cytoplasm of the whole biosphere will be
    revolutionized:

we'll live for all things living as a matter of course and hardly
notice a change when the time comes for ourselves to disappear.

SO THIS IS WHAT

So this is what is called the surface of a planet.
How unlikely a chance to have found so tiny a cinder-crusted
ember in the amazement of space. But here I am.
I'm running over thin snow etched through by an underlying pebble-

field where each pebble leaves a wake in the wind, or from orbit
I'm looking down on what could be high-latitude fault-block
mountains. Either way, it's incomparably strange to be alive, to be
confronted by such a dry, refractory facade, to be

at once so demanded and possessed of what one faces and so
detached, so indifferent to the charge and threat, so disposed
to flick one's own existence off one's cuff unexamined and without

regret. What I have come from is now an infinitesimal but still
bright and compulsively massive white hole in the darkness.
But there's no going back: the source repels, countenances no return.

I'm still moving too fast. I must slow down and begin again
in some crouching posture to strike one stone against another.

GATES

Gates. They're everywhere. Mostly invisible.
You've passed them before you notice.
Afterwards you find them closed behind you.
They're solid glass now—not a crack. We call them

regret. Safety also. They close you in.
They set you free. The old philosophers
wanted something better: all gates open,
no closures. They wanted it so earnestly

they called it eternity. They left us a certain
looseness in the hinges. Sometimes a gate
pulls an unexpected flipflop, makes you believe

there could be ways of wending all through the system
if you could find the right childhood day, a right
talisman to greet symbolic animals,

a right laughter, a rare windflower in sleep.

HOW COULD THEY

How could they be anything but elegies, those stories
of love between mortals and immortals? How can he but
obey and die when, seizing him reluctant by the hair,
she draws back his head, exposing to the approaching spear

that soft place where the neck throbs and armour does not reach?
How can she not shed tears, though destined to live
for ever and forget her mortal son, to see him at her knees
begging as when he was a child to have lights among the branches

lit once more, though tomorrow, as both know,
he will be dragged to death under chariot wheels?
These stars in this sky forget briefly how not to shine.

After their moment, there's nowhere to read them from. A few
fraying threads hold the book together. Already wind is turning pages
faster than you can see to remember even the most impassioned
    words.

THE FOURTH WALL

The fourth wall is invisible, as custom decrees. The pet
lamb wears a peasant smock. His namesake, the artist's son,
is equally well behaved. The family's unexceptional activities
are part of the work in progress. There's no seam where regular

mealtimes end and invention begins. Inside such installations,
    the artist's
children practise life. His wife is wiping her hands
on her apron, taking a few steps from a polka, arranging
snapshots. His daughter's wax crayons charge across the page.

There isn't room on a postage stamp for multimedia events
of this scope. That's why the usual borders had to be
dispensed with. The Prime Minister licks the stamp with special

relish. It is one of the nation's best loved artworks. The colours
are water-soluble and on rainy days, therefore, indistinguishable
from real people. How good for everyone when art smells of plain

linoleum, the sweat of young vegetarians, and melting snow.

As the Eyes Fail

As the eyes fail with age, one thing begins to look like another.
This takes you back to childhood and accounts for the growth
of visual metaphor in your later work—only now things are
    re-entering
the seamless identifications from which they emerged as the child
    learned

the names of particulars. Boundaries that separate give up in
    resignation.
The garden loses its distinct blooms and becomes a colour field. People
you believed you knew relax and merge into the figures that are born
exquisitely otherwise from dreams. History becomes more and more

a feat of let's pretend. And there's probably nothing you can do
    to resist.
It goes far to detaching you from the view that the world
exists in one preferred way. There's a method of putting the ways

together, but to make it work requires as many species as the
    biosphere
will sustain. And you've got to live through them all from infancy
to age. A casual spoonful of honey tastes of a million flowers.

LINE-BREAKS

Line-breaks are a crucial feature of the design.
Jagged ends secure entrance into the country of the muses
by radical surprise. Continuity matters too, and wholeness
of effect. Without those, broken branch tips

would have nothing to start and point away from.
There would be no tangy juice to venture beyond torn substrate
into an environing intelligential field.
To the rough scoriations themselves, unthought-of

natural graftings adhere, and thereupon begin to grow.
Eventually they constitute a new cortex redressing the old brain.
Lethal sports and dysfunction are common results, but out of these

premature severances evolve new species that prove viable.
The reader becomes lord of a forest rooted by and large
in disruptions. Strange beasts surround him from afar,

and even the snarling predators, growing progressively
heraldic, stand angelically at bay, enchanted by his song.

IT'S FITTING

It's fitting because it doesn't fit exactly.
It never did in the best traditions and in the last
analysis. And so, on these heady summer days,
she floats across campus in torrents of colour—a work of sheer

abstraction, all absurdity of matter and actuality
refined or defined away, as idealist or nominalist respectively
would put it. We see the point, but not as either this
or that. We've read her books carefully enough

to believe in a physics adequately real
to do justice to the metaphysics of her motion.
No doubt there's an art—and she has it—to enacting

the complementarity of fashion and animal vitality, a daring
to so debonairly taking up the breezy cause of chance,
dressing so liltingly in this envelope of indecisions

that she makes the shift from one exquisition to another
as effortless as June July and August.

ONCE ONLY

Once only in a million years can you expect a day like this,
and only one in a million passers-by gets a chance to taste it.
What blossoms were about is now turning red and round among
the leaves. Now you can see what those bizarre innovations—

literature in the vernacular, equal temper of the chromatic scale,
hermetic analogy, quantized fields, and negative
theology—made accessible. You're the only person in a leisured
class of one to be vouchsafed the momentary freedom to hold it

inside a single skin. Everyone else is drilling for oil, perfecting
the commonplace, coping with poverty or oppression, dying of
    redundancy.
On such a day, there's infinite space into which to expand,

infinite future, no foreseeable death that matters. The curve
    of the shoreline
commands forever; you'll reach a point at which you'll evaporate,
but no gate will slam closed; everything else will go on bending

through grace. In another million years, another one in a million
will be the subject of—or if he can't be, invent—a day like this.

WHATEVER ELSE

Whatever else they have in mind, builders of pyramids
bequeath us a symbol. What it's a symbol of may depend
upon a turn of phrase we apply to it. But whatever
it may become in print, it's a durable digression

from the desert of the unspecific—stubborn, local,
resistant, returnable-to, despite its floating
life in the mind. Vermicular cities encroach on these
concrete universals, but fail to consume them. Much of

the commerce there is a matter of turning familiar pebbles,
rubbing them from hand to hand, looking for a literal
embodying the magic of the figurative, looking for a figurative

owning the certainty and reassurance of the literal.
What with heat, flies, dysentery, one is rarely at one's best
when visiting the actual sites. One feels bound to compensate

by subsequent fabrication for what one missed at the time
    in the presence.

FRUIT WORMS

Fruit worms need a home too. That's why I never
spray my apple trees. In unsettled weather,
apples fall to earth with a parabolic and
satisfying thud. A person of genius

might hear therein confirmation of a profound
law of nature, an equation that, starkly simple
and admittedly approximate, takes the life-
span of a universe to see the light of day.

One's own death, however many times foreshadowed
and repeated, is rarely so easy as the thump
of apples. But in between, the views are often

ravishing, sometimes laced with the scent of
appley ethanol. The situation in the lab
is different. Most waking hours are occupied

reading up on published research, figuring out
ways of isolating preferred interactions,
assembling and testing apparatus, and easing

personality friction, to say nothing of
arguing for grants and recovering from years
of misplaced effort. But to make it all

worthwhile, from time to time an apple falls.

The point has been not to tell a story but to experience
how a story gets made. The historical record is abundant,
yet questions always arise—precisely about what is not included.
It's these questions that betray the motive for fiction, and it's clear,

is it not? that the actual can never provide enough data
    to preclude them.
Indeed, the more data, the more opportunity for a field of inquiry
and speculation to open between pairs of facts potentially related.
Given the passion of erstwhile seamless webs spontaneously
    to rift asunder,

it should be no surprise that reality may reduce to fewer and fewer
small islands in a turbulent foam of imaginary rhetoric.
That rhetoric itself harks back to a child's need for a syntax

before she has the parts of speech or names of things. You may
    find her
somewhere in your own memory scan, vocalizing as she tongues
her fingers in her mouth, while in another room a celibate illuminist

enrolls her in the usual chronicle of catastrophes
and renascences surrounded by angels of praise.

SIGNS

Signs of life are everywhere. It's over now,
but evidence remains. Something as simple as
post-hole patterns distinguish rectilinear
genera from exponential, paratactic, and heteroclitic.

Passing through fossil orchards, one can almost see
impatient nesting warblers tugging at apple blossoms.
But there was no hope for them: the pace of change
had grown faster than any generative

number sequence could try and err its way through.
Life went on, nevertheless, as our presence here,
back at the original sites, attests.

Life went on, but in an unpredicted form.
It was not foreseen that the old flash-flood beds
would survive, nor that such as we would return

to groom and race there a million species of genial urge.

SIGNS OF LIFE

Signs of life are everywhere. They are not,
as once was thought, confined to carbon chemistry
and consciousness. Wear-patterns and stretch-marks on the fabric
of tensor space provide evidence enough,

or a swaying branch after a bird has gone deeper
into the greenness of green or the blueness
of blue. Some other animals feed routinely on absence:
their not having been is their real and only life.

(I admit that mentioning them disrupts their habitat.)
A particular kind of snake grows from the tail forward.
When the head is complete, it begins with the tail

and eats its way along its length. As the last smack of the lips
is consumed, a final flick of the tongue inscribes
the tail in time again, and the process goes on.

Signs of life are everywhere. The garden
won't stop growing. When we turned our backs, moss,
heather, thyme, violets, forget-me-nots, and strawberries
took over. As gardeners, they've proved among the best.

The text goes on repeating itself: the walls
are made of it. The dead were the designated
auditors, but since we've ceased to believe in them,
it's become a way of life for the living.

He's the oldest monk. No one is left who remembers
when he first materialized at the gate. The finger-stops on his flute
are a sunny April evening after six days' rain. He plays

his own hills and valleys now, woods ways, waters ways.
The sacred books are pasture rocks against which
his sheep card their fleece into strands the length of the wind.

You ask

You ask what I'm thinking. I rarely know. So I make something up.
Oh, it's plausible on the face of it. But you sigh. It never
satisfies. You're part of the story, but not the end. For years I tried
    to think
like one of the mariners they speak of in the sagas. There was a famous

landfall recorded there. If I think long and steady—think
like one of those old-timers thinking like his ship—I'll be first
to come upon it again. And sure enough, the pigment of the old map
elutes, migrates, and draws a circle round the spot. Standing on shore

with some of the locals, not much is to be seen. But by good luck
or canny choice, you are an archaeologist and take charge of the dig.
Bit by bit it emerges—longhouses, boatsheds, rootcellar, forge,

a few stray implements and amulets. No grave goods—the
    settlers went over water
to die or to burial. And then finish. Roofs fell in. The venturers
    never came back.
Somewhere an old man—he gets to look more and more like
    me—bends

over a stone—he never stops—hammering bog iron into
    boatnails. It's of him
it occurs to me to tell you I'm thinking now—the rusting edges
    of his sweat
in firelight, a long scar across his eye. Where is he getting
    ready to go?

Do you hear? The warp and wrench and clap and crack of shiplap
    on a landless sea.

LOOKING BACK

Looking back, you see it turn to elegy; ahead, to apocalypse.
The garden is empty and delocalized; the city, a caustic,
    carbonized horizon
hard to articulate, and of besiegers and besieged few survive
to enter history and imagination. Of the unexampled cycle of stories,

all run down, even in the hands of the most devoted late redactors,
from sublime to fussy or facile picturesque. One escaped hero
dies on a foreign shore wondering whether the future will ever
    trace back
its mitochondrial DNA to the mother goddess who gave him birth.

Another becomes a missionary for the sea god far inland, where
    people
are at pains to work out how to interpret stranded flotsam
    of the salt, encircling
stream of life. Waking one day, the desperation of an alien planet

drives us so far within that we rediscover the garden,
    uninhabitable yet,
but so like the city of transparencies we hope to grow worthy of
that for the first time a kind of green, budding apple evolves

from the leaves, a long way from ripeness, but already blushed by
inexorable photons from a starry sky we may soon enscroll and adore.

PART FOUR

... a season of
flowering galaxies ...

It's time to talk

It's time to talk regenerative braking, the dark
matter that may close a universe. As I die,
a conviction—call it, if you like, another illusion—grows
that failure of life here complements attainment of life there;

that *rallentandos* here are twilit sisters of *accelerandos*
elsewhere; kinetic loss is potential gain; diminished
actuality, a chance for the virtual to accent itself;
that gaps are invitations; nothing will be left empty for long;

or, since emptiness itself is another kind of fulfilment,
that imaginary space is vibrant with probability
amplitudes; that everything is wriggling: now it feels like me, now

something else. Life on the river goes on. It is the season of flowering
galaxies. Tomorrow I shall be unavailable for comment. Another voice,
not necessarily speaking a language you will understand,

or even be able to hear, will answer when you call.

LIVING THROUGH

Living through the boundary-event, you don't notice it happening.
It takes millions of years to reduce to the fine line between strata
that you can publish. This morning is like any number of
other mornings—quick goodbyes, a few jokes about the weather—

but this is the day you don't come back from the outer planets:
a raised hand, a nod and a smile as you drive off are the last ever.
You aren't aware of miscalculation until you're into the final
    seconds of countdown:
somehow your adversary has got the inside track; as you circle
    the walls,

planning to dash for the Pristine Gates and safety, he is always
    between
you and your hope, forcing you to run the wider circuit. The
    pain in your side
gets worse slowly enough to remain endurable for years, then
    suddenly

a breakdown in function stops you from ever going up the
    mountain again.
You thought that to be felled in your tracks like this was what they call
death. It hadn't occurred to you that as the old ones retract,

a set of what turn out to be quite different sense organs push out
tendrils into a new universe that has lain embedded in ordinary

former things unrecognized.

GRAVITATIONAL CAPTURE

Gravitational capture is a rare event. That's why the planets
are so barren of satellites, despite the frequency of space-
debris. The empty potential orbits are a temptation
to some of the most meddlesome human proclivities. In time,

many circuits are occupied, and the sky becomes too noisy
for adequate observation. The result is fundamentalist astrology.
The perpetrators live and die in a hell of their own invention,
cut off from the opportunity of objective godhead and never aware

that all they've been doing is reading their own brain waves,
the severest case of self-enhancing feedback-looping conceivable.
One way of escape is to follow the threads of action that when

pressure is suddenly relaxed race outward along natural
micro-fissures in space and time, disproving perfect
felicity and feeding into a dangerously open

but more indubitably living universe than was ever imagined.

THIS GRAND CIRCUMFERENCE

This grand circumference in flight tells you unavoidably
that you are the centre from which it began long before your birth
and under conditions in which you couldn't have existed even
if you'd been there to try. It helps a little to say this

as you resign yourself to receiving no more than a trivial
signal from what once was close but now can be only a clumsy
attempt at revisionism, something knowably far from truth,
an almost-maximally-after-image. Everything between you and then

is stretched out to a fineness barely tangible. The ground
on which you cannot choose but shift from foot to foot—
     that too is creaking and
groaning as the veritable space it occupies expands. How
     deeply the activity here

derives from that very expansion is a pertinent question. This general
pulling-apart may eventually elicit the structure of nothingness itself,
of which there is more and more all the time, and from the
     contemplation of which

you may expect perhaps as much as you're likely to find

anywhere, and enough to satisfy your most errant desire.

OF THE INTERIOR

Of the interior, there's not a square inch of surface
that hasn't been wrought by some mosaic implantation.
Here and there emerges a recognizable form—a god, a creature,
a mathematical object. In these areas, there may have been

intent to communicate. Elsewhere, either the message is beyond
our capacity, or the purpose, if there was one, was not expression.
Daylight plays there and shivers into countless hues
possibly for its own sake only. Over the years, however—

so tenacious our obsession with such abstract spaces—
we've devised to impute desire and meaning to these too.
Hence, new ways of reading and the languages they presume.

How future tourists will interpret these antinomian cathedrals,
there's no predicting. Possibly, in ways unknown, the walls embody
habitual acts and passions from which, bearing strange witness,

we shall walk free, reconstituted, or theophanically misconstrued,
into the lives of our distant discoverers and heirs.

WHEN YOU COME TO THE END

When you come to the end of one chain of reasoning,
you flea-hop and hope to land in the middle of another.
The process is probably less arbitrary than it appears:
witness the survivability of the flea. The point is that

wearing the amulet enables you better to imitate the alien
animal it represents. It's not a matter of magic,
but of acquiring the characteristic prowess of other species
by successfully acting out the patterns of their behaviour—

which means thinking as they think. Alone on stage,
he is a bower bird; his virtuoso art elaborates a love
grotto to allure a potential mate. I stress again the courtship

is *in potentia*. As you know from your study of the bird,
the nest, if one is ever built, is elsewhere. The hidden
variables in the dodgy locus of the bat's adventure are the insect

prey for which she changes course. What to the casual observer
appears purely stochastic is thus, in truth, subtly determined.

Words lie

Words lie flat, but the world comes curved. Equations run straight,
but the world whips and lashes. The patient supposes the world
    a green cave sealed
behind a sheet of optical glass. To break the glass and enter
    would be to
break yourself. Ghost images buff that transparency as you watch

and weave before it. They dance across whatever you can see beyond.
The ends of statements have a habit of inverting their beginnings.
    But here,
what disappears beyond the left periphery re-enters as neither
    itself nor its inversion
on the right. There's a relation, but you can't pin down or pick it out—

a stretching or compressing of significance, is it, a stirring,
blending, unreeling, or unravelling? Wide awake, you still
see everything through the filmy texture of a dream busily at odds

with what it transmits. Floor levels warp. Perspective alignments
    tangle.
Every species repeatedly tears off sketches of its own definitive
    morphology,
mingled unashamedly with a little surdity, offset here or there by
    a skew

or so, or worried by a fly struggling in a web between the boughs.

COLD BOTTOM

Cold bottom water floods continental shelves. Or everything burns;
air is black with naked carbon. The freak alone survives.
He's the one with thick skin, feathers, eyes on top of his head
to warn of swooping predators, eats oxygen, grooves on altruism.

We're his descendants, alive because we learned to live
on exhaust gases. The additives and oddities that once made him
a pariah have become the norm: we actually think we're quite
    good-looking:
in fact, we've evolved a whole science to prove it's only

logical to think so. We're catastrophists at heart—with reason:
we've survived so many gross assaults and improvident
probabilities. And it's all there to be decoded from ten toes,

rosy and warm from soapy bathwater. They got the way they are
gripping the dust from old volcanoes. Then the shoemaker
    did his thing,
crafting journeys for them from soft animals whose kith and kin

were survivors too.

STAR-CLUMPS

Star-clumps in a spiral arm, macroproteins
on the surface of a cell, a spray of apple-blossom—
the softer the focus, the more numerous
the candidates. Absence of a scale also

multiplies the possibilities for metaphoric perception.
A homogenized mist at the end of the process
of defocusing means anything goes. It includes
all metaphors, but without sensory clues

you need an exceptional talent for indeterminacy
to extract them. That's why the convention is to retain
some semblance of external reference, even if

it's only fuzz on a peach, faint speaker hum
to signal the power is on, or caught breath that could be
someone's last, a dreaming child's, or a lover's sigh.

Standing on the rim, one looks ahead down the slope of the graph
slumping away under wind and gravity into a low moan below,
    while behind,
an old caldera basin speaks of a plateau in values of the state-function
in defiance of all the variables chattering beneath grade promiscuously

unaware of times past and to come. It took you undetermined billions
of years to get here, and yet, for all the unforeseeable accidents of
passage, the physiography of which you are now a part appears
disarmingly familiar, something close to the memory of a beach
    near the sea

in another universe disjunct from this and experienced out of
the impenitent passion of childhood. You kept the aliens at bay in that
earlier life, as you do now, by a sheer act of will coupled with

a correspondingly intense self-absorption. If you were to begin
    walking
downslope towards the clusters of populous mirage over the flats,
or back across the fossilized vulcanic lake, the dust under your
    feet would be

soft as phantom limbs of dead cyclopean heroes stretched out
    on the floor
of ancient afterworlds. Remember how you paused to speak to those
overwearied achievers and adventurers as you passed through
    their dispersed

ashes. Their whispered answers are just hoarse enough to give you
the friction that you need to make your way, though whatever
    they once meant
is as unintelligible now as the complement of stable hadrons that drift

through time building and unbuilding the open triumphs
of matter among
whose glades you move, swimming through interstellar dust
clouds, vanishing
in order to return, erupting from expedient to expedient,
laughing irreversibly.